GOLF 101
A BEGINNER'S GUIDE
TO THE GAME OF GOLF

BY
MARK R. RIVARD

Golf 101

Copyright © 2024 by Mark R. Rivard

ISBN: 979-8894790404 (hc)
ISBN: 979-8894790381 (sc)
ISBN: 979-8894790398 (e)

The Reading Glass Books
1-888-420-3050
www.readingglassbooks.com
fulfillment@readingglassbooks.com

CONTENTS

INTRODUCTION

If I were going to paint my house, cut my lawn, build a tree house for the kids or change the oil in my car, I first would get all my gear together, formulate a plan, then go about getting the project done. Why is it, when a person wants to learn golf, they grab a few clubs, ask a friend a couple questions, and go either to the driving range or a golf course and start blasting away?

Why do they ask someone who cannot break 100 to teach them the game of golf? And why would the 100 shooter say OK? I have played this game for 40 years, my brothers and I hung out at the course, at the range, caddied, followed the better players at the club around the course, listened to them talk in the bar, discuss technique on the putting green and in the parking lot. I have also given over 20,000 lessons and played competitively as an amateur and professional for the last 25 years, and yet occasionally, I am still puzzled by the easiest of looking shots on the course. Is it because I am stupid, or is this game really the hardest game ever created? I am tempted to agree with the latter. I have heard the best athletes of other sports say that they would rather roll their bowling ball, pitch their pitch, throw their pass under the most extreme conditions, than have to putt a four foot putt for the club championship. Why?

Golf is an individual sport. Other competitors are not the golfer's opponents, the golf course, the weather and the golfer's own spirit are the competition. Even good golf swings can look very different. Even as a team sport the golfer plays as an individual for his own score. If he plays badly, he can only blame himself. A golfer can try to blame someone else, but then why does he take all the credit when he plays well? The game is enormously mental. The golfer must only beat himself. But long before the golfer can beat himself, he must learn many details, odds and ends and another language. The following pages will give any golfer the tools to understand the details surrounding the game and concentrate on learning the swing.

BEGINNING GOLF

"I hit a drive and three iron two feet and made the putt for a birdie." How many times have you heard statements like this and known the people were talking about golf but did not recognize any of the words as you knew them? Golf has its own lingo and unless you play golf regularly or are around someone who does, it is very difficult to understand the game or even get interested enough to try it. Even if you do get interested, the mystery of swinging the club makes things even worse. So many would-be golfers are misled by the friend or spouse who shows them how and in the process actually discourages them from trying. Golf is not easy to learn, but anyone with proper instruction can learn it, regardless of age.

Most sports are reactive or live ball sports. In baseball, football, surfing and most other sports, the player has the chance to act naturally, to react to the ball, or the person, or the wave, or the curve in the road. The participant may move, scream, jump or hit back by moving his feet or reacting to movements directed at him. Responding instinctively makes any sport ultimately easier.

Golf, in turn, is a dead ball sport. The ball just sits there, daring us to do something to it. And golf fundamentals are often contrary to basic assumptions. If you swing up, the ball may roll on the ground. If you want the ball to go up, you must swing down. If you swing to the right the ball may go left, but it may also go right; the opposite is also true. The golfer must do it all, although he does get competitive relief when his adversary plays poorly. He still must play the golf course. Every aspect of golf is dead ball; the lakes, the hazards, the trees just sit there. Golf becomes a live ball sport only when the player's attention is diverted by his anger or by outside influences. For one to be good at golf, golf must remain a dead ball sport, and it does, as long as the golfer stays calm, using his mind's eye to create the shot needed. He must then create a swing that will produce the shot imagined. He must use his imagination as much as he uses his body. If the player learns the game only by making physical swings at the ball he will be limited by the stature of his physique. To learn and then improve at golf, the player must learn the basics of the swing, imagine the shot needed and practice with a target. The difficult aspect of golf is to apply these fundamentals to the shots needed on the golf course.

The purpose of this booklet is to get the beginner started in the right direction, not teach him/her how to play the game. It is a guideline for learning. It provides an understanding of the terms and makes discussions about the game easier. A golfer does not have to play the game to talk about it. People talk about football, basketball and baseball without playing. Why not golf? The combination of the aspects of golf discussed in this publication allows the reader to at least talk about the game in a reasonably intelligent manner, avoiding the embarrassment associated with being a rank beginner. It also allows the beginner a much better chance at enjoying a lesson.

Understanding how to make starting times, or how to drive a golf cart ultimately makes going to a golf facility much more relaxing. The familiarity of some basic rules and knowing something about etiquette helps the beginner to enter the world of golf with a better attitude. My hope is to instill in the new golfer the thought that golf is a game for a lifetime and can be learned a little at a time, and the information presented here is the beginning. Golf is a mysterious game. Hopefully, in the following pages we can unravel some of the mysteries.

CONCEPT OF GOLF

The idea behind golf is to move the ball, mostly via the air (though not always), from the teeing area or tee to a closely mown (green) area designated by a 6-8 foot pole (pin) into a hole. The tee area is designated by color coded markers indicating different levels of difficulty and allowing for different levels of ability. The ball is struck with a club and guided down the fairway (short grass). Trouble, rough, or hazards must be avoided to achieve a good score. The goal is to accumulate the fewest number of strokes throughout the round. Every stroke at the ball is counted, including missing the ball completely. Normally the game is played in groups of four, although not always. There are many types of competitions, but most people play for enjoyment.

There are 18 holes constituting a full round of golf. Each hole is par 3, 4, 5 and occasionally 6 strokes. Par on a hole is the number of times the golf ball should be well struck plus two putts. All 18 holes also add up to par 72, sometimes par can be 70, 71 or 73. The holes are normally a combination of 10 par 4's (40), 4 par 5's (20) and 4 par 3's (12). Playing only nine holes is common.

The majority of golfers shoot over par, while players shooting under par constitute only a small percentage of the golfers. The average serious male golfer plays to about 90 strokes, while the average female plays near 100. Most beginners play to about 120+ strokes for eighteen holes.

GLOSSARY OF GOLF TERMS

ACE: A hole-in-one. A shot is called an ace when the ball goes into the cup when struck from the teeing ground.

ADDRESS POSITION: The position the golfer assumes to set the swing in motion. Also called the set-up.

AIM: Although the golfer aims at a target, aiming correctly also applies to the first few feet in front of the clubface. The line must ultimately connect with the target. The ball may curve in the air or when it is putted on the green, so the golfer must take this in to account before striking the ball and aim accordingly.

BACK OF THE CLUB: The opposite side of the clubface

BACKSPIN: The spin applied to every golf ball struck with a lofted club. When the club is swung down to the ball and nipped cleanly off the turf, the impact imparts spin in the opposite direction of the swing.

BALATA: Softer cover golf ball, feels better but cuts too easily for most players. It will state on the ball box which substance is used.

BALL MARK: Indentation left in the green when the ball hits the green on the fly. If ball marks are not fixed within 24 hours the roots will die and brown spots will appear. Fixed within five minutes, it will repair itself in 48 hours.

BALL MARKER: Object used to mark the position of the ball on the green, usually a coin. When a ball interferes mentally or physically with another golfer's line of play the ball is marked.

BANANA BALL: A slice (see SLICE) flight takes the shape of a banana on its side, arching to the right (left for left-handers).

BELLY: Middle or equator of the ball.

BENT GRASS: A very fine blade creeping grass used on tees and greens, it intertwines to make a very smooth surface when closely mowed on a daily basis.

BERMUDA GRASS: Bermuda grass is used in warm climates because of its durability and resistance to heat. This grass turns brown, dormant, when the cooler winter temperatures arrive, it then turns green during the hot season. Many warm climate golf courses overseed with rye grass during the cooler months. It burns out when the bermuda begins to turn green.

BIGFOOT: Someone bigfoots you when they step on the grass between your ball and the cup on the green. This impression in the putting surface may deflect the putt.

BIRDIE: One stroke under par on a hole.

BLADE: Irons are also called blades. Like a skull, the leading edge of the club strikes the middle or belly of the ball.

BOGEY: One stroke over par on a hole.

BOGEY GOLFER: A golfer who normally bogeys most of the holes, shoots about 90 on the average.

BUNKER: A hazard consisting of a prepared area of ground, often a hollow, from which turf or soil has been removed and replaced with sand or the like. Grass covered ground bordering or within a bunker is not part of the bunker. Concerning the Rules of Golf, the margin of a bunker extends vertically downwards, but not up.

BURIED LIE: When the ball buries itself nearly completely under the sand.

CAVITY BACK: The depression or hole on the back of the iron clubhead. Material is taken from this space and added to the outside edges of the clubhead, or perimeter. This redistribution of weight assists in more solid hits. Also known as perimeter weighting.

CENTER: The solar plexus is considered the center of the swing. The clubhead travels in circle around this imaginary hub.

CHIP or CHIP SHOT: To hit the ball a short distance in the air. The ball spends most of its time on the ground and is usually hit from the fringe surrounding the green.

CHUNK: To hit the ground before making contact with the ball (FAT).

CLOSED: The clubface is aimed to the left when the stance is square to the line of flight (opposite for lefties).

CLOSED STANCE: The left foot, hip and shoulder are closer to the line of flight than the right foot and hip. The line of the hips or feet or shoulders aim right of the target

CLUBFACE: Parallel, horizontal lines visible on the clubface, usually eight in number. The ball is struck here.

CLUBHEAD: The combination of back, clubface and hosel.

CONCEPT: The club swings in a circle, from a center or hub, the ball gets in the way. Mentally, the swing plane appears in the form of a large wagon wheel, hand fan or pane of glass. The body rotates, taking the arms, hands, and club along for the ride.

DEEP GRASS: The rough grass areas bordering the fairway.

DIMPLES: Indents on the golf ball. Each equipment company has found the secret of flight based on the configuration and number of dimples. These dimples work against the air to give the ball additional lift and supposed better direction and backspin.

DIVOT: The club strikes the ground after contacting the ball, taking away an amount of turf.

DOUBLE BOGEY: Two strokes over par on a hole.

DOUBLE EAGLE: Three strokes under par on a hole, occasionally one on a par four, more often two on a par five.

DRAW: When a flying ball curves slightly from right to left at the target, preferable for most people.

DRIVE: Refers to the shot you hit on par 4's and par 5's from between the tee markers. It is not necessary to hit the drive with a driver (#1-wood); other long clubs are easier to hit and easier to control. Many average players and beginners hit the club they like off the tee for their drive.

DROP KICK: To hit the ground before hitting the ball. Many times a good shot can occur because the ground helps straighten out the clubhead and accelerate the club into the ball. This happens most often on a driving range mat

DUCK HOOK: A very fast turning or curving ball to the left.

EAGLE: Two strokes under par on a hole.

FADE: Opposite of a draw, a controlled curve of the ball to the right, also preferable to good players.

FAIRWAY: The short grass between the tee and the green.

FAT: Hitting the ground first before hitting the ball and digging up a lot of dirt; resulting in little distance.

FERRULE: Plastic ring around the shaft just above the hosel.

FINISH: The position the body takes when the swing is over. A good finish is when the weight is supported by the left foot and leg. The stomach and chest are turned to the target and the arms are raised high near the left shoulder. The right foot is near vertical.

FLAT SWING: A swing with the left arm and club shaft being below the point of the right shoulder at the top of the swing.

FLEX: Each shaft is rated for its flexibility, X (5) extra stiff, S (4) stiff, R (3) T-regular or medium, A-soft, A, or L-ladies. Some shafts of lower grade are not identified.

FLIER or FLYING LIE: The ball surrounded by grass acts like a launching pad not allowing the metal of the club to actually touch the ball during contact. The ball jumps out of this type of lie, usually with no spin and flies longer than normal.

FORE: After hitting your golf shot, it may sometimes veer toward another player. It is good etiquette to yell FORE as loud as possible to warn the player of an errant shot.

FORGED: Metal is heated and formed, and then excess metal is ground off to form correctly shaped clubheads.

FRIED EGG: The ball plops into a bunker in a small volcano shaped circle like an eggyoke surrounded by the white.

FRINGE: The short grass cut short like fairway only about two to three feet wide and rings around the green.

FROG HAIR: Short grass around the green, fringe.

GET UP AND DOWN: Getting the ball into the hole from near the green with one chip or pitch and one putt.

GIMMIE: A short putt that is conceded to the golfer by a playing opponent, it still counts. There are only gimmies in match play when the distance is very short or the hole is conceded to an opponent.

GOLFANEZE: Language spoken by many golf instructors using only golf terms, making it almost impossible for the golfer to understand what he or she is being told.

GOOD LIE: The ball sits on top of the grass allowing a good clean hit.

GOOD ROLL: A putt that rolls very easily toward its target. A good roll does not have to be holed, it could just be very close to the hole. It may look as if it is going in.

GOOSENECK: Another name for offset or hosel that has more curve than normal. Goosenecks assist in placing the hands ahead of the ball at impact, assisting in a strike of the ball with a downward motion.

GREEN HIGH: A golf ball lands along side the green, hit far enough but not straight enough.

GREEN SIDE BUNKER: Sand or grass bunker close to the green.

GRIP: Rubber or leather part of the club that people hold on to, also refers to the placement of the hands on the club.

HAZARD: Any bunker, water hazard or lateral water hazard. Bare patches, scrapes, tracks or paths are not hazards.

HEEL: Part of the clubhead just below the hosel. The shaft is inserted in the hosel.

HITTING ZONE: Twelve to twenty inches during the swing when the ball is being struck by the clubhead.

HOLE IN ONE: Very rare, compared to the number of golfers; almost always on a par three (eagle), once in a great while on a par four—a double eagle.

HOOD: To stand the clubface on its leading edge, delofting the clubface—making a 7-iron look more like a 3-iron.

HOOK: For right handers, curving the ball in the air too much to the left. Left handers hook the ball to the right.

HOSEL: That part of the club which connects the shaft to the heel of the clubhead-gooseneck.

IMPACT POSITION: At impact the body assumes a position of leverage to the back of the ball. The weight feels approximately equal to both feet. On the downswing the hips, head, and spine will slide slightly to the left before they uncoil and face the target. The weight is equal on both feet at impact and continues onto the left foot at the finish.

INSERT: Plastic or epoxy in the clubface of a wood made of wood.

INSIDE-OUT: The arms swing very close to the body on the downswing and down the line of flight through impact, creating the feeling of swinging out to right field on the follow-through.

INVESTMENT CAST: This club making process allows the manufacturer to pour metal into a mold, making all sets of irons the same. Previously, clubs were forged by hand.

LEADING EDGE: That part of the clubface which is the further most toward the target when the club is set down on the turf.

LIE: How the ball sits in the grass. A good lie is usually found in the fairway where the grass is very short; you can find good lies in the rough. Normally they would be considered fair, because clean striking of the ball is hindered by the longer grass. A bad lie is when the ball is surrounded by grass on all sides making it difficult to get the clubface on the ball.

LINE or LINE OF FLIGHT: The line of flight is considered to be the imaginary air path the ball will follow if the shot is made the way the golfer intends.

LIP: It is the edge of the cup or edge of the sand bunker.

LOFT: The slope up the clubface, long clubs are steep resulting in lower **shots**, while short clubs are more sloped creating higher shots.

MAJOR GOLF CHAMPIONSHIPS: U.S. Open, Masters, P.G.A. Champion-ship, British Open.

MATCH PLAY: Golf that is played hole by hole. A player wins when he is more holes ahead than the number left to play. A match can be over after the golfer has won the first 10 holes. The opponent cannot win with only 8 holes left. The score would be posted as 10-8. There are gimmies or conceded putts in match play. A player may concede a hole at any time.

MULLIGAN: An extra drive given on the first tee. Golfers are afforded this courtesy when they haven't loosened up. Mulligans are not permitted in the Rules of Golf.

NECK: Another name for hosel, woods made of wood have long necks wound with string to support the wood. Irons have hosels of metal: a.k.a. gooseneck, shank.

O.B. or Out of Bounds: A two stroke penalty. It is in the interest of fast play to hit a second ball if the golfer thinks his ball is out of bounds. The second ball must be played from the original spot.

OBSTRUCTION: Anything artificial, whether erected or left on the course, including the artificial surfaces of roads and paths. *(See the USGA Rules Booklet)*

OFFSET: Refers to the bend in the neck of the club. It puts the leading edge back from the target further, allowing the golfer an extra moment to keep the hands in front of the ball. Can also be called a gooseneck.

OPEN: Clubface is aiming to the right of the target when the stance is square.

OPEN STANCE: The right foot and hip are closer to the line of flight than the left foot. The line of the hips or feet or shoul-ders aim to the left of the target.

OUTSIDE-IN: The arms swing away from the body on the downswing and closer to the body at impact, feeling like a cut across the body. The swinging of the club sometimes takes the appearance of a looping motion as the club swings down and across the ball.

OVER THE TOP: This motion in the swing refers to the act of swinging the arms down and across the body and line of flight. This happens when there has been no shift of weight to the right on the backswing, resulting in only an arm swing, and shift of weight from the center to the left.

PGA - PROFESSIONAL GOLFERS ASSOCIATION: An association governing professionals, not amateurs. There is no such thing as a semi-pro golfer. Golfers are either amateur or professional and the associations governing these situations are well defined. Not all golf shop attendants are golf professionals. Golf professionals hold a Class A card. This means they have finished an apprenticeship under another Class A professional. The process takes approximately four years.

PAR: The score an expert should shoot on each hole considering two putts and full shots well struck. All of the par 3's, 4's, and 5's, also add up to PAR for 9 holes or PAR for 18 holes

PERSIMMON: Type of hardwood, aged and oiled, used to make fairway woods and driver heads. Hardly ever seen anymore—most "woods" are made of metal.

PIN HIGH: A ball struck toward the green ends up even with the pin on either the left or right.

PITCH: A short lofted shot, usually within fifty yards of the green, many pitches spend more time in the air than on the ground.

PLAY THROUGH: Allow faster players to play through by stepping to the side of the fairway in a safe place while the faster group coming from behind plays the hole.

PRACTICE TEE: Driving range-practice area where golf shots can be practiced.

PRACTICE GREEN: Putting green not connected to the course.

PULL: Hit the ball to the left with very little curve in the flight.

PUNCH SHOT: The golfer takes a more straight-faced club, chokes down the grip, swings easier, and hits the ball lower than normal.

PUSH: To push the ball right of the target on a straight line.

PUTT: Rolling the ball with the putter while on the green putting surface.

QUADRUPLE BOGEY: Four over par on a single hole.

RELEASE: The natural uncocking of the wrists on the downswing which allows the left arm to fold against the ribcage while the right arm extends down the target line.

REPAIR TOOL: Fork-like tool used to fix a ball mark.

ROUGH: The longer grass, not fairway, green, or tee.

ROUND, ROUND OF GOLF, or STIPULATED ROUND

OF GOLF: Eighteen holes, unless the committee determines fewer. Nine holes is not considered a round of golf unless stipulated by the committee. (*See USGA Rules of Golf*)

SAND TRAP or BUNKER: Not a play ground, it has been called sand box or cat box. After playing from the bunker, it is proper etiquette to rake the sand smooth. It is a two stroke penalty or loss of hole to the golfer who rakes or grounds his club in the sand before hitting. Grass bunkers excluded.

SCORING LINES: Parallel lines on the clubface.

SCRATCH GOLFER: A golfer who usually shoots par or better for 18 holes. There are very few club scratch players. Tour players are better than scratch, under pressure.

SET OF CLUBS: Combination of woods, irons, and a putter: A full set is 14 clubs-putter, sand wedge, pitching wedge, 9-iron through 1-iron, 3-wood, Driver (1-wood) or the golfer could use a putter, pitching wedge (equalizer, 10-iron, wedge,) sand wedge, 9-iron through 3-iron, 1-3-5-7 wood, or any combination of clubs, not to exceed 14 by the Rules of Golf. Each player decides which 14 clubs he wants in his bag. A good combination of clubs for the beginner or intermediate golfer is a 4-iron through 9-iron (6 clubs) and a pitching wedge, a regular sand wedge, and a high lofted sand wedge (for high soft shots around the green, (3+6=9) and a 1-3-5-7 woods, (9+4=13) and a putter=14. This selection will allow the average golfer a wider variety of golf shots on a regular basis.

SET-UP/ADDRESS: Positioning the body to strike the golf shot.

SHAFT: The round, elongated metal or graphite part of the club connecting the grip to the clubhead.

SHANK: The part of the club also called the hosel but more of the clubface is included. Also de-scribes a squibbling shot, hit on the same part of the club that veers to the right quickly.

SHOOT: The golfer does not shoot golf. You may shoot a score or a gun but the game of golf is played.

SHORT GRASS: Fairway grass length. "It's on the short grass; it's OK!"

SKULL: To hit, belly or blade the middle of the ball with the leading edge of the club resulting in a low line drive.

SKY: To pop the ball up in the air very high by hitting the ball on the top half of the clubface.

SLICE: Curving of the ball to the right; a banana ball.

SLOT: The feeling of having the club in exactly the right place at the top of the swing, which makes it easy to hit the ball. 90% of a good golf shot is the result of what is done on the backswing.

SMILE: A cut or gash in the cover of a golf ball.

SNOWMAN: Eight strokes on a hole, 8. Double snowman, 88.

SOLE: The part of the club that is considered the bottom when the club is placed on the ground naturally. There is normally an identifying number and name on the sole. The club is soled when in this position.

SOLE PLATE: The metal plate on the bottom of the woods which protects and covers the weight added to the clubs.

SPIKES: The metal cleats on the bottom of a golf shoe. Slang referring to golf shoes. Cleats today are made of plastic to protect the putting surface from being scarred.

SQUARE STANCE: The feet, knees, hips, chest, and shoulders feel as if they are all aimed in the same direction.

STEP DOWN: The ridges in the shaft where the shaft gets smaller and smaller from grip to clubhead.

STROKE PLAY: This match is played on a total stroke basis. Nearly all of the events on television are stroke play. The ball must be holed at the completion of each hole.

STRONG GRIP: Placing the hands on the club and turning them too far around to the right.

SUMMER RULES: The Rules of Golf state that the ball is played as it lies. Its position or lie may not be improved before hitting. Historically, golf was played this way, regardless of conditions.

SURLYN: Golf ball cover made of a material harder to cut.

SWEET SPOT: That part of the club that gives the best feeling of contact. When the ball strikes this spot, the clubface will torque neither open or closed.

SWING PLANE: The golfer swings the club in a circle around the body on an inclined plane. The circle is tilted to match the angle the body. If the circle were filled in with glass or some see through substance, it would reflect the 'plane' or 'swing plane' of the swing.

SWING WEIGHT: A way of scaling clubs to determine if the head weights are equal. Also determines if the clubs are heavy. The weights are measured B, C, D, E, and each category can very from 0-9. *Example:* D-3 would be an average man's swing weight while a C-7 would be an aver-age woman's swing weight. The B weights are used for children's clubs. A matched set can be 1 or 2 points off and still be considered matched.

TAP-IN: Short putt of 12" or less.

TEE, TEE BOX, TEEING AREA or TEEING GROUND: The beginning area of each golf hole. This area will be marked by color coded tee markers.

TEND THE FLAG: To hold the flag in the cup prior to and during an approach putt. The flag must be pulled once it is held. Two stroke or loss of hole penalty if a ball hits the flag, when putted from a position on the green.

TIMING: The word refers to the order of the swing. To time the hit of the ball correctly, that is to offer the most amount of power with the least amount of effort; the golfer must allow as many parts of the body to participate as possible. Swinging easily and getting the club in front of you as soon as possible on the downswing accomplishes this task.

TOE: By comparing the clubhead to a person's shoe, the toe of the club is where one's toes would be, the heel is in the opposite position, and the sole is the bottom of the club.

TOP THE BALL: Swing and only graze the top of the ball resulting in a rolling shot along the ground.

TOP OF THE GRIP: Refers to the area of the grip on top when the leading edge of the club is ninety degrees to the line of flight. Designs often designate the top of the grip.

TOP OF THE SWING: The point at which the club has reached the end of the backswing. The longer clubs are usually parallel to the target line and many times parallel to the ground. The shoulders are 90' or more, causing the middle of the back to face the target, 70% of the body weight is on the right leg and foot, the left heel is an inch or so off the ground, the left knee is pointed forty five degrees behind the ball, the hips have turned forty five or more degrees and the tilt of the spine is to the right or behind the ball.

TOURING PROFESSIONAL: Tour professionals play golf for a living. Most golf professionals work in the trenches, managing golf shops, selling clubs, and giving lessons.

TRIPLE BOGEY: Three strokes over par on a hole.

UNDER THE LIP: A ball flies into the sand bunker and gets stuck under the sand at the edge of the bunker.

UPRIGHT SWING PLANE: When the left arm and club shaft are above the point of the right shoulder at the top of the swing.

U.S.G.A.: The United States Golf Association, the governing body of amateur golf are also the writers and interpreters of the Rules of Golf. Sponsor such tournaments as the U.S. OPEN, U.S. AMATEUR, WOMEN'S U.S. OPEN, U.S. SENIOR AMATEUR, U.S. SENIOR OPEN and eight other national championships for amateurs. Rule booklets, written and distributed by the USGA may be purchased in any golf shop. Don't try to memorize, keep it in the golf bag for use when a question arises.

WATER BALL: An old ball used when there is a chance that you might hit your shot in the water. A lot of average or below average golfers play this way. It gets expensive to hit new balls into the lake all the time. Check the USGA Rules Booklet regarding changing balls during play.

WEAK GRIP: Placing the hands on the club turning them too far to the left; can cause an extremely awkward swing. Shots to the right are normal with this grip.

WHIPPING: The strings that appear to hold the wood head on the shaft. Actually the head is held on by glue, and sometimes a little set screw. The whipping supports the neck of the club and helps keep the wood from splitting. It is also more pleasing to the eye.

WINTER RULES OR PREFERRED LIES: *(USGA Rules Booklet)* Adverse conditions are sometimes so general throughout a course that a Committee believes that moving the ball to a "preferred lie" would promote fair play.

WHIFF: To miss the ball completely with a swing, it counts as a stroke.

WORM BURNER: Topped shot or ground ball that zips along the ground.

DEEP CREEK

RULES OF PLAY

1. Golf carts must use the 90 degree rule.
2. 100 yard markers, 150 yard markers, and sprinkler heads are measured to the center of the green.
3. Pin Position: Red Flag - Front of Green.
   White Flag - Middle of Green.
   Blue Flag - Back of Green.
4. Please repair ball marks, replace divots, and rake bunkers.

DEEP CREEK GOLF CLUB

DESIGNED BY

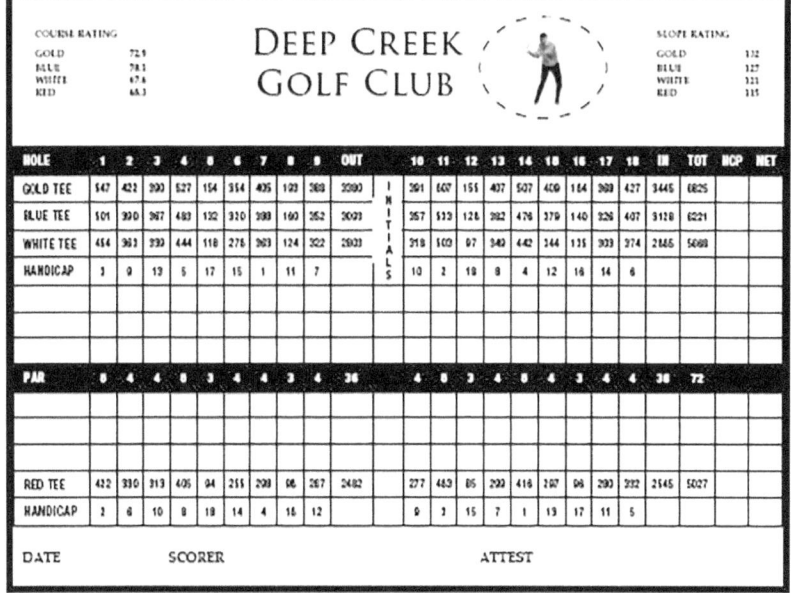

DEEP CREEK GOLF CLUB

COURSE RATING		SLOPE RATING	
GOLD	72.9	GOLD	132
BLUE	70.3	BLUE	127
WHITE	67.6	WHITE	121
RED	68.3	RED	115

HOLE	1	2	3	4	5	6	7	8	9	OUT		10	11	12	13	14	15	16	17	18	IN	TOT	HCP	NET
GOLD TEE	547	422	390	527	154	354	405	123	368	3290	I	391	607	155	407	507	409	164	368	427	3445	6825		
BLUE TEE	501	390	367	483	132	320	398	160	352	3003	N	357	513	128	382	476	379	140	326	407	3128	6221		
WHITE TEE	454	363	330	444	118	276	363	124	322	2903	I	318	100	97	349	442	344	115	303	374	2446	5068		
HANDICAP	3	9	13	5	17	15	1	11	7		T	10	2	18	8	4	12	16	14	6				
											I													
											A													
											L													
											S													
PAR	5	4	4	5	3	4	4	3	4	36		4	5	3	4	5	4	3	4	4	36	72		
RED TEE	422	330	313	405	94	255	298	66	267	2482		277	483	86	299	416	297	96	290	332	2545	5027		
HANDICAP	2	6	10	8	18	14	4	16	12			9	3	15	7	1	13	17	11	5				

DATE   SCORER   ATTEST

READING A SCORE CARD

Look at the front and back of the score card on the previous page. Not all score cards look exactly the same but all have the same basic information. This particular score card is very basic, although it does have a few special instructions and a map of the entire golf course. Start in the upper left hand corner and work your way around the score card...

COURSE RATING: Even though there is par, the course is also judged or rated on its degree of difficulty. The color refers to the tees that are played. The higher the number the more difficult the course. This system is based on the yardage of the course. The longer the course the higher the rating. This course plays 4.6 strokes harder from the gold tees than the reds.

SLOPE RATING: This is another system of rating golf courses. This system assigns each golf course a rating by degree of difficulty. Each golf course is rated in ten areas. A course with 5 bunkers on every hole may get a 10 rating in bunkers, but because the greens are flat and not too large, making them easy to putt, the greens may get a rating of 5. This is a much more accurate and detailed course rating system. The course and slope rating is determined by a committee appointed by the state golf association. The committee travels from course to course, rating each by a list of criteria.

HOLE: The numbers in the row refer to the hole number you are playing while the larger numbers under each numbered hole are the distance in yards. Par 3's are usually 240 yards and less. Par 4's range from 275 yards to 470 yards. Par 5's range from 470 yards to 620 yards. Longer holes than that are par 6's, but you don't find too many of those in golf. Lengths twenty five to fifty yards shorter are used for women.

GOLD TEE: Also known as the championship tee, sometimes called the tips, because that is as far back as you go on the teeing area. Playing from the tips normally makes each hole play at its most difficult position. These tees can also be called the tiger tees. You will hear people refer to the golf course they played as the gold tees, or the blues, black or the tips.

BLUE: The next most difficult position from which the golf course can played.

WHITE: Normally known as the men's regular tees. Most golf is played from these tees. Many of the LPGA (Ladies') Tour events are played from the men's white tees.

HANDICAP: Handicap has many meanings, in this case it refers to the difficulty of the hole being played. Each hole is assigned a handicap based on its difficulty. A Bogey Golfer will need a stroke to tie a Scratch Golfer on these holes, although one's handicap does not ensure a par or a bogey.

The seventh hole (1) is the hardest hole to make par on while the twelfth hole (18) is the easiest. The word handicap in golf also has another meaning. Each player is also given a rating or handicap. To establish a handicap, a golfer must belong to a country club, a golf league, or golf course mens' or ladies' association. The golfer must play a regulation round of golf, eighteen holes.

Occasionally, nine hole leagues do establish handicaps for their membership's convenience. Every time the player turns in his score card to the golf shop, the course rating must be selected, usually by a circle. These scores and course rating are recorded by the golf pro or handicap chairman on a posting sheet. The posting sheet is then sent to the state golf organization or handicap company. The lowest ten of the last twenty scores are used to compute a handicap. Some courses will have the posting sheets in the ladies' and men's locker rooms and the golfer may post her/his own scores. These figures are computed and returned to the clubs on a monthly basis. The golfer designates the course played by circling the rating which applies. If there is no circle the golfer will be assigned the white tees course rating.

The slope system of handicapping is a little different. Using this system a player actually is assigned an index of 4.6 or 15.8 based on his scoring averages and course rating. This index is then plugged into a floating scale which changes based on the SLOPE RATING assigned to that particular course. Golf shops normally have written information on these systems.

OUT: The numbers directly under this word refer to the total yards at the end of the first nine holes, many times referred to as the front or the turn, also designated as the total yards of the front nine.

INITIALS: It is easy to transpose scores between players. This particular card has room for the players initials to make it easier to get the scores in the correct place.

IN: The front is played OUT, or out in 45. The back nine is played IN as in to the club, or in 44 for a total. In this space is also the total yards for the back nine.

TOT: This stands for total, OUT in 45 and IN in 44 is 89. This space also designates the length of the eighteen holes in yards.

HCP: When establishing a handicap with the state organization or club, an identification card with the correct handicap will be issued. The actual handicap should be written here. The handicap can then be subtracted to give the player a net score. A handicap may change on a monthly basis, which will be posted at your home club. The ID card from the state organization will provide space for the monthly handicap and a space for the organization official stamp. This stamp will be used by either the golf professional or the handicap chairman.

NET: Gross score minus handicap equals NET SCORE. This information only tells you if you have played near your handicap or have beaten your opponent after he has also reached his net score. This allows a player of higher caliber to compete with a player of lower. Golfers can wager on the net scores. The better player can give other players the difference of their handicap. This difference can be noted by circling the more difficult holes listed in the HANDICAP row on the card. The circled holes designate where the higher handicap player gets strokes from his opponent in match play. In stroke play the strokes are given on each nine. Normally players wager on the outcome of each nine and the total eighteen hole score to create three separate games. This type of wager is called a Nassau.

PAR: This is the number of strokes the golfer should take as an expert, good and sometimes average golfer. All of the par 3's, 4's, and 5's, also add up to PAR for 9 holes, the turn, or par for 18 holes.

RED TEE: Ladies tee markers and yardages.

LADIES' HANDICAP: The ladies golf course is much shorter from the red tees. Sometimes this changes a hole drastically, even changing the men's long par four to a ladies par five. This type of situation changes the difficulty of a hole so the golf course is rated separately for the ladies.

DATE: Date ensures correct use of the last ten scores.

SCORER: Many times golfers play for prizes or wager small bets while they play. Honesty dictates that another person keep score.

ATTEST: Signed by another player to ensure accuracy. Many club tournaments are won by good players who keep a false handicap. This practice is known as sandbagging.

Deep Creek Golf Course also chooses to give the player a map of the course. They also ask the player to use the 90 degree rule. This rule asks that all players drive the carts off the path only at right angles. The player should drive the cart along the path until he reaches his ball. The players may then drive straight across to their balls and return to the path in the same manner. By allowing minimal golf cart driving on the grass areas golf courses can maintain a superior condition.

Since golf is played by measuring distance, information is provided by placing stakes, marking trees, or placing discs in the ground at 50 yard intervals. The markers are measured to the middle of the green. Some golf courses put the distances on the sprinkler heads, which are located at random throughout the golf course. These measurements are done two ways, either to the center of the green or to the front edge of the green. It is best to ask the golf pro if it is not stated on the card. Color coded pins also tell the player the location of the pin relative to the center of the green. The difference can usually be one or more clubs longer or shorter, depending on the pin's location. Many people may hit a 5 iron 150 yards. Let us say the golfer is standing at the 150 yard marker preparing to hit his shot when he notices that the pin is colored blue. An average green may be 90 feet deep or 30 yards. The given distance is 150 yards and the player estimates that the pin is about halfway back of center. He can now split the green in half, 15 yards on each half. Split again and add 7 ½ yards to make a total of 157 ½ yards to the pin or a 4 iron instead of a 5 iron.

It is common for a golf ball to leave a dent or ball mark, also known as a pitch mark, in the surface after it flies to the green. This unrepaired pitch mark will turn brown and die within 24 hours. This ball mark can be repaired simply by pushing a golf tee or a ball repair tool into the edge of the indent and prying the center of the indent back and upward. Work the tee around the indent until it is gone. Then tap the turf down lightly with the putterhead till smooth. This practice is considered good etiquette and players should get into the habit of fixing two or three ball marks per green. If left unrepaired the ball mark will take two weeks to heal. If fixed immediately, only 48 hours.

When practice swinging or hitting a golf shot, many times turf is lifted up by the leading edge of the golf club. This flying dirt is called a divot. It is proper etiquette to replace the divot and step it firmly into its original hole. Many golf courses provide sand or a mixture of sand and top soil and some-times grass seed in containers attached to the golf carts or on the tee of a par three. This mixture should be put into the divots. It is good etiquette to fill in holes that other golfers have neglected.

A courtesy to other golfers is to rake the sand bunker after playing the shot. It is tough enough to hit the shot out of the sand let alone play from someone's footprint.

Many golf courses may also give the following information on the back side of the score card:

PLAY WITHOUT DELAY: Don't waste time. Play as fast as possible, 2 hours for 9 holes is considered good, although there is nothing wrong with playing faster, 1.5 to 1.75 hours is possible.

CARTS ON PATHS AT ALL TIMES: Many courses provide cart paths and they require the golf carts are kept on the paths because the carts can damage the grass when used excessively in the same areas. Some course allow the carts almost anywhere except on the tees, greens and in the bunkers, but be careful of turning too sharp and digging the turf.

DRESS CODE ENFORCED: Golf has a tradition or history which many golf course owners and operators find nearly sacred. It is best to assume that regular type golf slacks, sport shirts, mid-length shorts, and golf shoes are preferred rather than jeans, running clothes, tennis clothes, or beach attire.

OUT OF BOUNDS or O.B.: White stakes to the left or right of the rough. If the golfer hits the ball beyond these boundaries or loses his ball he must play another ball from the original spot. The players are allowed no more than 5 minutes to look for a lost ball in all cases.

WATER HAZARD or LATERAL WATER HAZARD: Red or yellow stakes mark the boundaries of these water hazards. There are many instances of how to play these hazards. (*USGA Rules Booklet*)

EMBEDDED BALL RULE: Many golf course are watered heavily, or built in rainy areas and when the ball hits the ground it plugs and has to be dug out and cleaned to hit properly. When the ground is soft from rain or watering, there is no penalty and you may clean the ball and drop it as close as possible to the spot where the ball lay, under the Rules of Golf.

USING GOLF CLUBS

If you have a set of clubs, get them or borrow a bag of clubs from a friend and take them out and look at them as you read this section. You should familiarize yourself with the tools before you attempt to use them. Be careful not to swing them indoors unless you have a 8x8 space with a 8-9 foot high ceiling. Don't swing unless you are sure there is no one close to you!

Golf clubs have specific uses. Obviously a putter is used to putt or roll the ball along the ground. A sand wedge is used to blast the ball out of the sand. The sand wedge may also be used from the grass. The pitching wedge is for pitching the ball at any time to the green, as far as one hundred twenty-five yards for a better golfer or for a short pitch shot. Sometimes a pitching wedge is used to move the ball the into a more convenient location, such as pitching the ball safely out of the trees. You may also pitch the ball with a sand wedge or any club in the bag. You may also chip with any club in the bag. Pitching and chipping are terms used to describe an action, not the club selection.

The wedges, 9, 8, and 7 irons are called short irons because they are short in length and hit the ball a short distance. Depending on your caliber of golf, short irons can be hit any-where between 65 and 165 yards for full shots.

Most beginner's hit the 9 iron 60-100 yards. It will go further as your skills improve.

The 6, 5, 4, irons are the middle irons and hit the ball middle distances from 150 to 200 yards, but remember, you may also pitch or chip with any of these clubs. The 3, 2, 1 irons are the long irons. Some players can hit their 1 iron 240 yards or more. Long irons are not good clubs for the beginner or intermediate as the straight faces connected to longer shafts make them more difficult to hit.

The driver, or #1 wood, is used from the tee markers. The better golfer gets the length advantage while many times the average golfer will find himself in trouble. Some skilled players use drivers off the fairway to reach par 5's in two shots. The fairway woods—2, 3, 4—are used for distances longer than the long irons but many times the 5, 6, 7 woods replace the distance of the long irons. Hitting the 2 & 3 woods requires a good lie. Utility woods such as *Gyro Seven, Adams Tight Lies, Cleek,* or *Baffler* have runners on the bottom which help the club cut through the heavy grass and turf easier. They normally have the loft of a 5, 6, or 7 wood.

Sometimes, golf shots are refered to by their club or flight pattern, such as: Drive refers to the shot hit from between the tee markers. Wedge refers to a pitching wedge hit to the green and 7-iron refers to a shot hit with a 7-iron. So, you can slice your drive into a bad lie in the rough and dig a baffler out 50 yards from the green and pitch a wedge in close to the pin but push the putt, leaving a tap-in for a bogey.

GETTING THE BALL AIRBORNE–MENTALLY

Golf shots are NOT lifted or scooped. Golf shots with irons six through the sand wedge are com-pressed or squeezed between the ground and the clubface in order to make them rise. Conceptually, woods and longer irons strike the inside back of the ball. At least, this is the visualization a golfer must use to get the ball airborne. Another useful thought is to think of the ball being hit at the bottom of the swing, not on the way up. The most common error among all golfers is to help the ball upward by scooping or lifting.

Setting or soling the club properly on the ground contributes to the correct image in the golfer's mind. If the club is soled improperly, or aimed in the wrong direction the golfer will visually try to lift the ball, get the club under the ball, or be urged by his subconscious to swing in the direction the club aims. Simply aim the club properly and swing in that direction.

All of the clubs, when soled properly, are designed with the grip angled slightly ahead of the club head toward the target. This setting of the club should give the impression the ball is being squeezed against or compressed into the turf. In reality, you are only returning the club to its original design during the motion of the swing, most golfers don't. (Like hammering nails with the wrong side of the hammer.)

Soling the club properly contributes extensively to the concept of the swing. These mental images remind the subconscious what is correct and counteract the mistake of scooping before it takes place. A good teacher will introduce the mental/conceptual aspects of the game the moment the golfer takes their first swing; then there will be no future surprises. Many bad habits become ingrained and the horror stories of bad lessons revolve around the entrenched ideas the golfer has taught himself.

Learning the game's mental and physical attitudes are essential to improvement. The golf swing is never always physical or never always mental. It is always a combination of the two, it could be 99% mental and 1% physical, the opposite, or 50%-50%. The type of shot the golfer faces determines the percentage. Curving golf shots, higher or lower than normal shots and many shots around the green and in the bunkers may require more imagination. Shots from the middle of the fairway at 150 yards may be more physical in nature because practice of this type of shot is more repetitive. Although the mental side of the game is extremely important, as a beginner the game may take on a more physical nature-the swing must be learned. Once learned, more attention to the use of the imagination becomes the goal.

It was earlier stated that the club must be soled properly for the tool to be used properly. For instance, most mishit shots by golfers of all levels are the result of not returning the club to its original design at impact-scooping. Most misdirected shots are due to poor aim. To sole the club properly each club must be looked at individually. The angle of each clubhead to the shaft predicts where the clubhead and ball should be placed in the stance before hitting.

The position of the hands is almost always just inside the left thigh. For long or short clubs the location of the ball is moved left or right in the stance relative to the length and lie of the club. The shaft is connected to the clubhead at a slight angle, the angle being greater for the shorter clubs. Soled correctly, the grip on the wedge is angled well left of the clubhead. This shorter shaft causes the club to be swung more downward than forward causing the ball to be struck at a much steeper or downward angle than a 5-iron. The 5-iron, a middle iron, is struck at a much steeper angle than the driver. This is why irons take divots and most woods usually don't. This is also why an iron club has a much more pronounced leading edge—to facilitate taking turf. The point where the leading edge strikes the ground is actually in front of the ball.

The longer clubs, being of flatter lie come into the ball less steep and contact the ball very cleanly, but the ground is usually struck after the ball is hit. The ball, when struck correctly is always hit slightly below the equator and on the downswing. A shorter club will take more of a divot, although a punched 5 iron may take a divot like a 9 iron.

With the driver the hands are still ahead, but only slightly, which means that even the driver is hit with a slight down motion. Because the hands get back to the ball a moment before the club does, the club must go downward before it can go for-ward. The most powerful drives occur when the clubhead path is exactly parallel to the ground at impact, a very difficult thing to do consistently. The weight of the clubhead is directly behind the ball allowing a precise hit and delivering the blow with the club's true loft. This ability to return the club head to the correct moment of impact is determined by the movement of the body. If the body motion is off, the clubface will be off. In other words, the motion of the body, the movement of the arms and the club itself must work together. It takes years to perfect the motion of the body in the golf swing, just as it takes years to perfect any motion where timing is critical: such as ballet dancing, swinging a bat, playing piano, or quarterbacking. In order to perfect these intricate motions, they must be taken apart, studied and then put back together. Each time, details are added to make the movement more solid. It is a lifelong process that will enable the astute student to look very natural in the end. Learned naturalness is the goal. This is the learning process and it is discouraging at times, but if the student understands the process, it will be easier to accept small failures and keep marching forward. There are no lasting quick fixes.

Remember, all clubs are basically the same, so your conceptual view will work with all of them, keep studying and eventually the technique will work. This is a building block method of learning, patience is essential.

USING THE PRACTICE OR DRIVING RANGE

The best way to groove your swing after a lesson is to go to a driving range and practice what was taught. The range is a place where the golfer can get into his own world and not have to worry about score, hazards or suffer from fear of embarrassment. Ranges vary in size; an average practice area is 250-300 yards long by 75-100 yards wide.

Most ranges sell practice/range balls by the bucket or bag. There may be small (30-40 balls), medium (50-60), large (60-80) and sometimes extra large (90-120). Every range is different. Some ranges have tokens purchased in the golf shop and inserted into a machine near the range and some golf shops sell the balls already in a bucket or bag.

Some clubs leave the balls in piles at the hitting spaces. Ask an attendant or starter the correct procedure. These balls are specifically designed for range use; it is considered poor etiquette to use them on the golf course. There is usually a rope, a row of golf bag stands or tee markers to mark the area from which to hit. It is proper etiquette to hit only from the designated area, as the tee positions are rotated regularly to allow for grass growth. It is also dangerous to hit balls a few yards ahead of the markers. The person to your left and behind you may hit the ball sideways into you.

Many people walk out to the range, buy three buckets of balls and stand there and smash them until exhausted. Remember one thing; the range helps, but only by having something to practice can a student learn.

There is a reason for this. If a person stays out there long enough, he will probably start hitting the ball better. Instinctively, the golfer finds ways to hit the ball and does not necessarily change something in the swing for the better. If it works on the golf course, congratulations! You have learned how to concentrate on the driving range, but in most cases it is only driving range rhythm. If hitting the ball OK on the range and bad on the golf course happens to you-Driving Range Rhythm, try taking a 10 minute break, sit down and review your basic thoughts during practice sessions. Pick one feeling in the swing and incorporate it into the full motion. Make full practice swings with half power before hitting balls. If you can't hit them at all, quit and go home. Come back another day and start fresh with full slow practice swings.

This suggestion counteracts driving range rhythm, which is usually fast and furious. It is too difficult to play golf with a fast furious swing. Things happen fast enough. The golfer must first slow everything down before the swing can be fixed. Slow down on the practice swing, step up to the ball and try to duplicate the practice swing with a ball in front of it. Some extremely good players say that they wish they could always use their practice swing on the ball. Practice slow control; power will develop.

Many driving ranges have rubber mats with green plastic carpeting and a rubber golf tee sticking up through a hole. When hitting from the mat, be careful not to build up false confidence. Golfers get their swings going so fast that they lose all feeling. It is possible to hit the mat behind the ball causing the club to bounce-drop kick-into the back of the ball. Some of these shots are fantastic. When seeing the ball fly so beautifully, a false sense of security builds. A drop kick is the same as a fat shot and on the golf course you will do nothing but hit the ground behind the ball. Go slow, use the tee provided and pay attention to the feeling of the ball being struck.

Unfortunately for women golfers there is plenty of free advice floating around the driving range. If you do not want free help, purchase a "Do Not Disturb" sign and hang it on your golf bag. If the "helper" still offers, point to the sign and explain that you are taking a series of lessons from the pro, "one pro is enough, thank you."

DRIVING A GOLF CART OR CAR

When arriving at the golf course, you will have the options of carrying your bag, pulling a hand cart, or renting a power cart/car. Many golf courses require the use of power golf carts, although you will find, as a beginner, it is much easier to walk because of the frequency you hit the ball. For most of us, walking is much more pleasant form of exercise. An eighteen hole golf course is between three and four miles. If the carts are restricted to the paths you will probably get the same amount of exercise because beginners spend more time getting in and out of the cart, walking to the ball, than actually playing the game.

The cart has an ignition switch or keyhole on the dash or just below the driver's seat. Make sure the key is turned to the 'on' position. Some carts have forward and reverse on the ignition switch; just turn the key to the appropriate position and the car is ready to go. The cart will move as soon as the accelerator is depressed. Most golf cars or carts have a buzzer or bell or some noisemaker as a reminder for reverse. There are usually only two pedals. The accelerator is on the right and brake on the left. Some carts have a third pedal to lock the brake when the cart is stopped. Newer carts have a half pedal on the brake pedal itself and when pushed forward locks the brake. Always use it coming to a stop. When pushing the accelerator the brake lock comes off. Tapping the brake pedal again also re-leases the brake. Some carts have gas engines and some are electric. If you can't hear the engine, it is electric. Be careful not to drive away in the cart as your playing partner is getting ready to hit; it is distracting and may unnerve him. Many carts also have an automatic hill brake that engages when you get up from the driver's seat. The driver's seat is spring loaded. The cart's brakes will be damaged if the cart is driven with the seat up; it is also dangerous.

Power carts are like little cars and dangerous when overloaded or treated as a toy. Always use common sense when driving a golf car. Here are a few tips: Carts can be difficult to handle on wet grass going downhill. They should not be driven closer than thirty feet to the green, bunker, or lakes. Pull carts should be left about 10 feet from the green and not rolled on the fringe. Be careful of steep hillsides and steep downhills. Carts are made to carry two golfers and children without driver's licenses should not be allowed to drive. Some golf courses have an extra rack which will hold a third golf bag, which allows a threesome to use the cart and take turns driving. Don't forget to "buckle up the bags" on the cart! Some exclusive golf courses have caddies who will carry the clubs or drive the cart for the golfer.

REGISTERING TO PLAY GOLF

It is always advisable to call the golf course, or starter's booth before going to play. To help organize the day's play many golf courses require starting times. These starting times are spaced at 7-10 minutes apart. Eight minutes is common, the times stop at :56, restarting on the hour every two hours. For instance: 8:40-8:48-8:56-9:04-9:12…10:00 or 9:56-10:00, allowing the starter a few free minutes at the end of each hour to catch up or use as a starter's time. Most starters will give the closest time possible to the time asked for; ask for 9:00 and he will respond 9:24 or 8:48—meaning that everything between those times is taken. The busy courses, 200+ rounds per day, expect golfers to play as foursomes. As a two-some, expect to be paired with another two-some. Remember, everyone, even the pro was a beginner at one time or another, so don't worry about your level of play. It is a good habit to tell other golfers that your handicap is 40 or above if you are a beginner. Things will go along very smooth if others know what to expect. Also tell them that you have a playing strategy. "I move quickly, I do know the basic rules of etiquette, I'll be ready to play when it is my turn and I will pick the ball up when I reach double par. Please concentrate on your own game and don't worry about me, I understand how difficult this game is and I won't be a beginner for ever." Double par on a hole is a good time to pick up the ball and 'surrender'. "I will also place the ball about 15 feet from the cup on the green, so I can get a feel for putting."

The person furthest from the hole should play first. The person with the lowest score on the previous hole should tee off first. If that person is not ready, hit out of turn. As long as you move quickly and know when it is your turn, no one cares how you score. And if they do, it is their problem.

When you register in the golf shop, either pay for all the players at once or wait for everyone to arrive. Don't be afraid to ask the procedure and come back when your group is ready to go. It saves time for everyone, and you'll feel more confident if you are familiar with the procedure.

Checking on a starting time, ask the whereabouts of the starter. He is usually the one who has the most accurate list of players. Do not carry your clubs into the shop; accidents can happen. Look for an area where clubs seem to be stored: bag rack: leave the clubs there.

The better courses will have bag attendants. It is common to tip them $1.00-$2.00 per bag for their help. Many of these helpers will clean your clubs if you ask. You may also get your shoes cleaned in the locker room for a couple of bucks. Many municipal courses do not offer these extra services, but resorts and country clubs usually do.

Remember score card, pencil, tees, golf balls and a damp towel. Check the brand of balls you are using, you don't want to get them mixed up other players. A few pen/pencil dots near the numbers will designate your ball. Ask if carts are mandatory and if they must remain on the path. Ask the average time for eighteen holes.

BUYING EQUIPMENT

Don't buy a bag full of the most expensive clubs on the market just yet. It is more important to buy clubs that look good to you. You will only know that by going into the golf shop and looking at several different sets. It is OK with many shops to demo new clubs, so ask. It would be very difficult to explain all of the details of the types of clubs offered, so I will only mention a few design features.

Offset irons are easiest for beginners to hit. Notice the little curve or gooseneck in the hosel of the club. This gooseneck/offset places the hands slightly ahead of the ball at impact. This position creates a descending blow-the opposite of a scoop. Ask the sales person to show you the difference. Buy irons that have a medium amount of offset, a good metal shaft, a cavity back, and rubber grip. The cavity back or perimeter weighted irons are called so because metal is taken from the back of the club and distributed around the out-side edges or perimeter of the clubhead. This leaves a small depression or hole on the back of club. This particular design allows for a larger sweet spot, giving more solid feeling shots even when mishit.

Metal woods, that is, woods that are made of metal in the shape of a woodhead, are made by many companies. Their features are all relatively equal. The heads are usually hollow which allows for a larger sweet spot. Again, have the sales persons explain the benefits of the different brands. The features are very similar, but the prices may vary.

Graphite shafts are numerous. There are so many varieties that it would take another book to cover it all. Less torque or twist is the basic characteristic of a graphite shaft. When the ball is hit on the heel or toe of a club, pressure on that portion of the club causes the shaft to twist, opening or closing a few more degrees. These few degrees can cause the ball to fly even further off line, maybe even out of bounds or into a lake. Talk with the people who sell these items daily, as technology changes so fast that it is difficult to keep up with it. Buy clubs after talking to three different shops, or go shopping with a spouse or friend. If you think someone is going to surprise you with a set of clubs, somehow suggest that you would like to shop and be fitted. They can still get you a gift certificate.

A beginner's first set of clubs should consist of a medium size golf bag, shoes, glove, one dozen surlyn balls, two dozen tees, a ball mark repair tool, 4-9, PW, SW & 1, 3, 5, 7 woods and putter. Rent such things as a pull cart until you decide if you really want one. Many people prefer carrying a light golf bag with a minimum amount of gear.

The most important aspects of fitting clubs are grip size, length and lie. Determine your glove size and buy the glove first. Standard men's grips fit men's regular glove, men's medium large, and ladies large. Although a ladies medium size hand with long skinny fingers may like the feel of a men's regular grip. Just ask questions like, "I have to wear a large ladies golf glove, should I have a larger grip than most women?" If you get a 'no' answer, go to another shop-they are not aware of the grip importance. Don't let a salesperson convince you that your large hand will be OK on a small grip and vice-versa. Holding the club correctly is an important aspect of the swing.

The hands, when holding, must be able to work naturally. As a beginner, you don't need to create your own problems, golf is difficult enough.

The lie of the club needed is determined by the length of the golfer's arms. Long arms on an average frame will mean that the golfer needs a flatter lie and possibly short clubs, short arms-more upright and possibly longer. Ask to be put into the Ping measuring device. It is color coded and saves time and explanation. A knowledgeable pro can translate Ping color codes to any brand of club. People should not automatically get longer clubs or more upright clubs. These features are determined by the length of the golfers' arms. Ask questions about arm length in all shops, don't buy until the questions are answered sufficiently. If you are really worried about being fitted correctly consult a golf club repair expert.

For metal woods, wood covers or protectors are not necessary, but as a decoration they are nice. Some players like to protect graphite shafts with wood covers that have long knitted necks on them. Iron protectors are only necessary if you would really like to keep your irons looking new for a long time. Most people lose a few of them and end up with a 1/2 set of iron covers in a few months. The little dents they receive from clanging around in the bag do them no harm. You only need soap and water and a towel to clean your clubs. A hand brush with some soapy water will clean the grips-towel dry. Your first golf bag should be a small one that is light and easy to handle.

The best place to buy equipment is from the local PGA Professional. He is an expert, has been around the business for most of his life and knows a lot more about equipment than the spouse or friend. Trust and buy from the PGA Professional. If his suggestions seem out of whack, then seek another pro. They are in the business because they love the game and their intention is create goodwill. They want golfers to play their course, take lessons and buy from them in the future. They will steer you in the correct direction.

GOLF SHOES

When picking a pair of golf shoes, sometimes called 'spikes' because of the cleats on the bottoms, notice two little holes on either side of the tip of the spike. These holes match up with a spike wrench and allow replacement of worn out spikes. Spikes are sold in all golf shops or locker rooms for about 25-50 cents each. The cleats or spikes are in the shoe to keep you from slipping. Buy a spike wrench when buying your first pair of shoes, take out the spikes, Vaseline the threads and tighten them as snug as possible. Vaseline will keep the metal from rusting. You may also want to consider changing to plastic spikes, which many golf courses now require.

Wear golf shoes. Hitting from side hill lies or wet grass is difficult enough with golf shoes. The first time on the putting green in new golf shoes remember to pick up your feet. Many beginners and some long time golfers forget that the spikes protrude about 5-7 millimeters and drag their feet across the green, leaving gouges in the putting surface. The putting surface regenerates itself quickly but these spike marks make putting surface irregular and difficult to putt. Tungsten steel spikes last a long time but tend to create more spike marks than a soft steel spike when they become old. After holing out, look around the cup area and tamp down all the little spike marks. It makes it easier for the next golfer to putt.

Some people say, "get them a little small, they will stretch out". Bad advice! Get them fitted, and they will feel better and last longer. You are going to be walking around in them for 2-5 hours and if they fit improperly, you will hurt your feet and the shoes. If you play a lot of golf, get two pair, rotate them and let them dry out before using them again. Golf professionals own ten or more and many times get good sturdy leather shoes and use shoe trees after play. Usually, a soft a pair of tennis-style golf shoes will suffice and can be purchased for $30-80 in most golf shops.

GOING TO A GOLF RESORT

Make golf reservations at the same time as room reservations. It is always a good idea to make all of your plans 3-4 months in advance or sooner if possible. It is much easier to secure preferred golf times if you plan well ahead. 9:00 a.m. is prime time and difficult to get at the last minute. I could always tell if someone didn't know much about golf when they called two weeks before their stay and asked for a 9:00 am time on Saturday and were disappointed because it was not available. The same was true when the person asked if they could play as a two-some in the middle of the morning. Many resorts will allow that, but you must pay for a foursome; resorts have a large investment and must get as much revenue out of the golf course as possible. It is to your advantage to plan well in advance. If you must play as a twosome, plan on playing at daylight, or dusk. Ask in the golf shop if that is possible. It also helps to travel as a foursome or eightsome, twosomes and odd numbers make it difficult for the resort to accommodate your needs. If you don't mind hanging around the driving range or putting green, many times the starter will work you in when there is a no show.

Many resorts also cater to large business outings. Management will book them two years in advance. Many large groups will block two to three hours of times to accommodate their people. Don't get discouraged if your needs can't be met a month in advance.

When guests arrive, most resorts ask that golfers leave their clubs with the luggage, and they deliver the clubs to a storage area. There is usually a daily storage charge. Get a bag tag for your golf bag and put name tags on the golf shafts for identification. Always inventory your clubs after each day of play and after using the driving range. If a club or two is lost, they are much easier to find and identify.

If you want extra service in the golf department, tip the cart/club attendants and golf starter and learn their names. This little extra, $1 to $2 for cleaning each bag of clubs each day, $5 to the starter on the first day of play, insures that if you need a favor, earlier or later starting time than you have made, he will probably give you the favor over somebody else. People often need last minute changes and several groups will ask for that kind of help. Small gratuities will help you get around the resort easier than the next fellow.

Many times the golf staff has lived in the area for a long time, and can help with entertainment suggestions. If taking lessons from a pro more than once, it is a nice gesture to invite him to join you for a drink or dinner. Expect to pay or tip for the privilege of playing with the pro. If it is not appropriate, he will decline the offer.

SPECTATOR GOLF

If you are lucky enough to attend a professional golf tournament, you will never forget the experience, especially if it is a major championship. The best procedure is to buy the weekly book of tickets. Remember the practice rounds! They are actually the most fun rounds to watch. Many times the pros are actually just playing a game with one of their good friends/competitors. During this kind of match, they usually have fun and will talk with the spectators. It is a better time to get an autograph or say hello to one of the players if you may have a mutual friend. Many players will talk and joke, hit a couple extra shots, or extra putts. Don't expect the same pro to be so friendly once the tournament proper begins. These guys are at work when the competition begins and do not want to be distracted. Most tournaments are won or lost by a few strokes. They really don't blame the spectators, but it is part of golf etiquette to allow them to do their job.

When competitors are about to play their shots, stay very still, do not talk. Cameras and cell phones are prohibited during official competitions. Expect to park the car and ride a shuttle bus to the golf course. Parking costs $3-$4 and is a short ride from the course. Spectators are not allowed to wear golf spikes. Soft-soled, aerobic, or walking shoes are the best.

USING THIS INFORMATION

Learning the game of golf can be downright discouraging at times due to numerous theories and so many things to know. This information will help form a concept base that allows the golfer to feel comfortable with learning the game from a competent instructor.

As a warning, don't expect to just pick up a golf club and make contact. There are few natural golfers. There are people who learn easier than others and there are those who have an extremely difficult time learning the game. The latter have an improper conceptual view. They cannot let go of the idea of guiding the ball up and out to the target or they firmly believe the ball must be murdered. They thought they understood the idea behind the swing, but lifting, guiding and swinging hard are exactly wrong. There is nothing wrong with swinging hard as long as it is rhythmic; the real essence of a good swing is to under-stand the concept behind the motion.

As you take lessons and practice, ask questions about your swing. The best way to learn anything is to ask for the information. You will play golf for your entire life and the information in the beginning will form the concepts on which you base your learning. The knowledge presented here will get you started in the right direction.

So, take it, use what you can, take lessons, and play, but most of all, relax and enjoy yourself.

THE AIM CHECKER

Very few people actually aim correctly. The Aim Checker is especially helpful on short putts, chips and pitches.

Aim any club at your target.
Have a friend drop the Aim Checker in front of the club face.
Step away and look down the arrow.

The Aim Checker: $7.50 (plus 1.50 s/h)
To order go to www.theputtingtemplate.com

For more information email:
mrivard@theputtingtemplate.com

You can leave a message at: **866-977-3113**

THE PUTTING TEMPLATE

The concept behind the template is much like a good golf swing, the pure putting stroke should follow the turn of the shoulders. In the putting stroke though, the only body rotation is that of the shoulders. The template concept also involves the grip and arm connection to the upper front portion of the chest. When done properly, and with correct setup, the putter head will follow the lines of the template and return to square at impact. To concept also realizes that the ball must be struck crisply on the sweet spot to make the ball roll correct online. The golfer must also aim accurately so that the ball will always start off in the correct direction.

The four page instruction and descriptive pictures that comes with The Putting Template explains in detail how and why the template will cure your putting woes.

Comes in two pieces

Dimension 22 x 8 ½
Written instructions included
Fits in most golf bag side pockets
Secures to the green with golf tees

The Putting Template: $30.00 (plus 9.50 s/h)
To order go to www.theputtingtemplate.com

Professionals and Golf Shops can order 8 or more at $16 each.

For more information email:
mrivard@theputtingtemplate.com

You can leave a message at: **866-977-3113**

www.ingramcontent.com/pod-product-compliance
Lightning Source LLC
Chambersburg PA
CBHW050908120626
46554CB00003B/1070